As Are Right Fit

As Are Right Fit
Copyright © 2024 BENJAMIN S. GROSSBERG
All rights reserved.

AS ARE RIGHT FIT
BENJAMIN S. GROSSBERG
ISBN 978-1-957248-35-6
Harbor Editions,
an imprint of Small Harbor Publishing

As Are Right Fit

Benjamin S. Grossberg

Harbor Editions
Small Harbor Publishing

Contents

As Are Right Fit

You have begot me, bred me, lov'd me; I
Return those duties back as are right fit.

—*King Lear*, 1.1.99-100

My Mother's Dying

It is hers, and I am to have
none of it. A privacy. A whisper,
knees clasped to chest. A novel
on a long flight during which
she does not sleep
while those around her do.
Her face cupped in her hands.
Arms folded in, palms tight
to the biceps. Or chin
tucked to the chest. She hears me
asking for it but does not wish
to be impolite. She turns her back,
carrying her plate to another room—
fork gentle against its porcelain.
Solitary by an open window, she closes
the pages of her dying
when I walk in. She lets
the pen of it drop, folds
the paper over when I enter
the kitchen, when I see her
at table, writing
her dying. When I come to her knee
as children do, she puts her hands
in her pocket, brings up
a Mento or a plastic container
that shakes out M&Ms,
but I know it is in there, too,
her dying.
        Then, turning, she
asks if I will bring her

muffins, with bran, though
she cannot remember the word
bran, and raisins. Cannot
remember *raisins* but wants
she says a lot of them. I take this
for what it is: a measure
of flour, eggs broken
one by one into a bowl
and the whisking, a parcel
of her dying, the smallest
she can part with. It will rise, golden
over foil cups. It will fill my house
two hundred miles north
with its good smell.
I will bring it back to her,
her dying, and watch
for a smile, perhaps
only because she's glad
to receive it. Such a terrible thing
to part with this intimacy.
Even to her son. Even,
just for a few hours, to her son.

Her Charm Bracelet

circa 1957

Sweet sixteen: a heart with those words
cut into it. That must have been the occasion
for the gift. A tiny camera: ingenious button
on top, you press it and a door opens in front—
pop-out muzzle, a diamond-chip topped
close-up lens. She liked taking pictures—
seventeen, a Polaroid on Coney Island beach?
A mezuzah with a hole in back
through which you glimpse actual

parchment and a hint of ink: *Hear O Israel,*
the Lord is one. And graduation gifts, two:
diploma scroll, *Beth Jacob, June '59*,
and a mortarboard hat with a pearl on top
affixing the tassel, the whole thing maybe
the size of a penny. Almost eighteen,
about to meet my father, to elope. Then,
engraved, the silhouette of a child's head:
Daniel, 11.10.62. And that's it. That's

the last. But there might have been
three more head silhouettes, each
with dates, the next two in rapid
succession. And a fifth, too, made
not of gold but of some alloy that doesn't
reflect light. There might have been
another graduation hat—this one
a nurse's hat, starched platinum. And
a bingo marker—a peridot, pale green

on its sponge end, for the times her fist
gripped and stabbed hard then shot up
as she shouted *Bingo!* her voice a shattering
that made me start from my book into
glistening eyes. Might have been
a menthol cigarette with a ruby tip,
and a book charm, gold paperback
with raised silver letters spelling *King*
or *Koontz* for long afternoons spent

alone. Might have been a bottle, Absolut
brushed silver, a television with a knob
that really turns, and tiny knitting needles,
fluted and dangling for stationary decades
on the end of a couch. And also
a tiny couch, silver crumbs under
its cushions, and a scale obsessed over
that you could press with the tip
of your thumb, to make its little arrow move.

And a second heart charm, this one
with a too-fast ticking, its bottom half
necrotic, blood-starved—a charm part
gold, part hardened carbon. And lastly
a small gold foot with, at the pinky-toe edge,
a blood-stone chip—dazzling, malignant,
metastatic. And all of these dangling
on a seven-inch looping of gold
that her father hands her

on her sixteenth birthday, the crowded
jangling laid on cotton in a cardboard box,
and her protesting correctly that it is

too much, too heavy for anyone's wrist, but
since it is a gift and does contain real gold,
that she tries on anyway and turns
in the light and admires, sort of
admires, its strangeness and particularity,
when no one is looking, her mother

bringing to the table a grocery-
store cake alight with sixteen candles,
her father and brother starting to sing.

Pre/Post

1. They Suspend the Propofol Drip to Assess Consciousness

and, ghoulish, the body rises toward us. Its eyes wide, up-peering, its mouth open, hands swaddled and gripping at air. We know it has come back for us, but we do not know from where. Now from its face comes a rasping against the tube down its throat, its teeth arranged around the tube like petals. A rasping as the grip finds a hand. The nails biting in. It is my hand being gripped. The nurse, who is trying to untangle the tubes that trail the body, places the other hand in my other hand, and it locks on. For a moment, I am bent face-to-face with the body as it heaves up with all its weight. Its eyes are earth-fresh hunger, the balls pushing through the sockets. Sounds are coming from my mouth, too. I am saying the names of people in the room. Then *better* and *calm*. And *soon*. Behind me, someone says *love*. Then the drip begins again. The body slumps back to the bed. The grip slackens. I lower its hands to the stomach and release them into their own loosening. The body becomes dead still, though the eyes continue—upward, unfocussed—to gape. *She will remember*, the nurse says, motioning us back from the bedside, *none of this.*

2. The Bone Plug Fit Back On

like the top of a jack-o'-lantern. The skin—which had been shaved and peeled—folded back over to cover it. Then staples to hold everything in place. But for a few hours, it was exposed: brain and the thing other than brain, the corruption of cells broke loose from the pinky toe— explorers navigating to the top of their world and nestling there, growing fast and big as Jack's beans, having found just the loam they needed. But gone now, gone, *with*, the surgeon said almost laughing, *no brain attached.* That night, you sit up, sipping juice through a straw your husband bent toward you, eating half a cheesesteak one of your kids brought, glad—so you said—your Monday shows were on. Meanwhile, bone knits toward bone, and brain shakes off trauma like a pursued, tumbled animal that gets up and immediately resumes running. Over the next few weeks, we'll see you have your memories, but no numbers. You have the Coney Island house where your kids were born, the layout of rooms, but are wildly off about the years; can name the kids but—

asked just after—have no clue how many they are. From your bedside, Dad grips your hand. *It's all right*, he says, *she doesn't need numbers.* When the speech therapist holds up a clock, you stare a full rotation of its longer hand before you shrug. Then you lean in for the next question. The second hand continues to turn.

Trying to Bathe a Kitten, My Brothers Drown It

circa 1969

In an alternate universe, the kitten skitters free,
up the sides of the tub and out to the hall.
Its wet paws track prints on the hardwoods,
and its terrified rage through the house
ends in a crevice no boy hands can reach.
How they seem, then, the hands' small grabbing
underneath a low chair,
the boy faces compressed against the carpet
into strange rubber masks,
and the hands extending out,
snatching at the kitten
which presses itself shivering into the dust of the wall.
In an alternate universe, the boys get bored.
The kitten curls there
until the mother returns home, and it is to her
the kitten comes, to the turning of a can-opener crank
and the burst of tuna that it tentatively comes.
The three boys are outside now with a ball.
They are chasing each other through the woods
behind the house. They are shouting and running.
Maybe one is pushing another down.
Maybe one is crying, while the other two laugh.

I Sit at Her Bedside

back in the hospital

As you might roll up your right-hand sleeve past the elbow.

As you might get down on your knees, then on all fours, to lower your torso to the road.

As you might reach into the cold soup of a drain, into its darkness, so your hand, your forearm get lost to it.

The fear you might feel, the vulnerability of your hand when it hits water and you brush shapes there, some

with squared-off edges but others jointed, knobbed that might—how to know in the sway your own hand creates?—be moving.

As you might feel the grate against your cheek as you relax into it, accepting the asphalt against your hoodie and jeans, trusting

the brother who is standing by your legs where they protrude into the street, your brother who is ready to wave away passing cars.

As you might feel the grate, accept the asphalt, and trust your brother, but all distantly, your awareness focused now in your palm, its mute seeing, the fleshy inward of your palm in its waving, its reaching and swaying, and the feel of water in its beaching on your forearm, chunky with shapes, spindly, curving, that might be living.

In a moment you will come up with it in your fist, white ball dripping brown water, its red stitching hard as a scar.

In a moment, cage the ball in the fingers of one hand and raise it high above your head, a deft gesture that will elicit a jump and a *fuck yeah* from your brother,

or you will linger on the road till his big toe nudges your ankle for a third time, a fourth, and he says again, *The hell with it, let's just go.*

As you might glimpse him then: pant legs, dusty cuffs, antsy; as you might see his gray Nikes still paint-stained from when you did the house last summer, might see him where he calls from the dry, bright world.

Go if you're gonna go, you'll say. *It's here. Got to be here. I'm not going home without it.*

Vigil

1.
I believe you are there. In flashes, in the chamber
of your head, you are there.

This is not sentimentality, but an extrapolation.

I believe you spark intermittently. I believe the gathering
we understand as a consciousness. Intermittently.

I believe you come to yourself with only the company
of yourself in a vast silence: you

slumped at an interior wall, in pinprick moments
apprehending darkness

and your own breathing. I believe in those moments
you do not love us less, but do not think of us.

I believe the question of your own thereness
is too strange to allow

other concerns. As a sudden magnetizing
pulls from interior seas

the currents of you, as, for an instant, you coalesce
understanding distantly

self, self suspended in the echoing
hall of a body. I believe, before you disband,

the bursts of awareness that will never
come again, that are you.

2.

The eyes open, but there is no seeing.
The eyes open for a while then they close.
The eyes open, the irises move with the slowness
of a moon across the sky. The hands rise.

The hands rise. If you hold a hand there,
they grip it. You will feel they are warm,
their fleshy give. You will feel the nails
bite your skin and start at their strength.

If there is a soul, the soul manifests in the grip.
I believe there is no soul, but if there is a soul.
I believe in the grip and its ability to speak
as a soul. In the closing of the grip on a hand,

if there is a soul. In the marvel of warmth,
in the marvel that the warmth of a hand

can warm your hand.

3.

Mother, come to us out of your dying.

Mother, breach the surface

of your dying, let it drip from you,

your head, your right hand rising.

Mother, shake it from your face,

as after laps, early morning.

Give us one moment

in which we may see you

as you, your face, your hand rising

above the surface of your dying.

She Pulls Closed

the right parenthesis
of her dates like a car door.
Engine rumbling, she sits
waiting in the driveway for my dad
who has, as usual, gotten wrapped up
in putting something away,
or is simply in their foyer
at the painstaking work
of tying his shoes.
She is, as she never was, my mother,
patient in her puffy down jacket,
her pocketbook on her lap.
But why shouldn't she be? Engine running,
there's music, Night Ranger's "Heart's Away,"
and good heat, too.
She's comfortable in the thick seats
of the old Buick Regal,
a shade of brown she called taupe,
comfortable as she waits for him
late on a gray November afternoon.
He'll be coming soon.

The Poem as an Act of Betrayal

Who was she, that woman who died, who suffered
brutally and died? The pathetic lying-in-bed
woman who stole your voice with her wind-torn
vocal cords and croaked out my name? That woman

didn't eat or wash herself, couldn't be bothered to get
up or well or a grip. She trailed plastic cords,
tangles of them, had an open tube that ran across
her body, directly into her chest, had a tube under

her gown and more than half the time one
thick as a garden hose down her throat. That woman's
fists were claws when in delirium she tried
to thrust her way out of bed; nail pressure

bit into the flesh of my palm as I coaxed her
down. She smelled in a way you'd never smell
and had no taste for fine things. She wasn't a Fendi-
from-the-loose-crook-of-her-elbow swinger, didn't

know Burberry from blueberry, and no one
brushed her teeth. Let me tell you a story
about that woman: I read her four chapters
of *Pride and Prejudice*, and she didn't smile once.

She didn't, as you'd have done, put a hand
to her chest and bat her eyes, didn't repeat
Mr. Darcy Mr. Darcy Mr. Darcy with breathy roundness,
the bellying out of a nine-month pregnancy, didn't

find even the prospect of a ball delicious.
You'd have had no use for that woman.
You'd have sat with me on the edge of chairs
the nurses brought in, eating wedges of the cake-

size chocolate chip muffin that woman wouldn't touch.
You'd have sat there for half hour or whatever
was minimally polite, then zipped up your puffy down
jacket and swung your Fendi, barely waiting till we were

through the doorframe to shake your head, make
a dismissive gesture, and whisper *If we hurry we
can still make Bingo.* Let me tell you another story:
once, in Gatwick, a man passed us, old man,

thin, wispy-headed, bent, and you put your long-
nailed fingers on my forearm and said *That man is about
to die.* I barely had time to look back before we passed:
people and their luggage rushing along, but not

this man, slow, painfully slow. We weren't ten feet
beyond him when we heard his bark and collapse.
His face, you said then, *gray as cardboard.* You'd seen it
before, in your nursing days. That woman, the one

lying in bed, was her face gray, too? I bet I could
call you—any time I wanted, right now—and ask.
I bet you'd pick up. You'd put down your paperback,
take a schlook of some clear liquid that could strip

varnish, and tell me more about what you saw
on the nursing floor. *Gray,* you'd say, *gray as lint,*
as you rummage through your Fendi for a cigarette.

Her Gowns

Bar mitzvahs, a couple of weddings.
I was there when most were chosen,
there for the taupe silk with sashes
falling from each shoulder, crossing
in back. At the third fitting,
she left in tears because, she said,
it didn't drape right. A son's
wedding just days away. You can't
see anything wrong in the pictures.
It falls around her in scrolls as if
she'd stepped from a frieze of victory:
Juno raising a glass at the marriage
of a favorite. That reception was
the last time she let them lift her—
as Jews do—on a chair, four men
in suits parading her around
the dance floor, her arms raised.
My bar mitzvah: a knee-length skirt,
puffy, girlish sleeves. My eldest
brother's wedding, decades later:
a black jacket, long, off the rack,
intended to obscure. They all hang
now, a cast-off line of selves, chapter
by chapter, her textile biography.
She was 48, my age, when she wore
the taupe silk. I reach in the closet,
lift it from its hanger, and hold it up,
its worn-once fineness, feeling a cool
shimmer on my forearm, bring it
right against my face. Or imagine

doing that from a few hundred
miles north, only imagine it. She was
buried, as it is written that Jews
must be, in a plain cotton shift.

The Auction

circa 2010

There'd be a thing, I'd be looking at a thing
on a table in the auction, a thing on a table of things.
Okay, let's say it was a cup, and I'd be holding it,
looking at it. And she'd come over from somewhere
in the aisle, grab the cup from my hand, and lift it
toward the guy on the other side of the table, the guy
whose junk it was, and she'd say, *A dollar?*
with a question mark, but also with a period. *A dollar.*
And if the guy took too long to respond, she'd say
it again louder. But let's say he didn't, let's say he said—
holding up three fingers—*Three.* Then she'd say
not to me or to the vendor, exactly, not even but almost
to God, she'd say, *It's not worth three dollars.* Then
You want it? And before I'd answer, she'd reach
into her special purse, just for the auction, stuffed
with singles, and pull out two dollars and say
two, her voice at this point the flat of a shovel
smacking frozen ground: *Two.* And maybe the guy
would say *Three dollars, lady,* and she'd pinch
the shoulder of my t-shirt between thumb and forefinger
and start walking, dragging me, or he'd say
Okay, two dollars and she'd say, *Okay, wrap it in paper,*
and if he didn't have any she'd reach into the wire cart
she dragged behind her and pull out a wad of newspaper
and wrap the cup herself then shove it low in the cart
so it wouldn't break. She'd start walking again,
which I understood as my cue to follow.

The Wedgwood, the Watches

Wedgwood didn't matter, she says,
speaking to me in a dream. The little vases
and ashtrays, the boxes littering the house,
I ask, they didn't matter? No, she says, swirling
ice cubes in a tumbler of vodka, no, though
haggling for them at yard sales, watching
people wrap them in newspaper, then shoving
them so-wrapped into my purse, that mattered.
She takes a drag on her cigarette like she used to
at Bingo when I was five, six, seven years old
and she sat across from me, smoking cigarette
after cigarette to the drone of numbers in a hall
so dense with smoke you couldn't make out
blue hairs five seats away. What about watches,
I ask, knowing my mother's predilection
for watches: a Hamilton! she'd cry. A Seiko!
It still works! Winding its gear between
the long nails of her thumb and forefinger
and thrusting it right up against the side
of my head so I could hear the tick. Watches,
she says now, so ghostly in my dream
that she flickers as hazy and insubstantial
as cigarette smoke—smoke generating
smoke—didn't mean shit, she says, slicing
the air with the edge of her palm like she did
when she was alive, her face, her jaw
set firm. But showing you, showing Dad
the watch after I came home from the auction,
holding it out and watching for the tick
to register in your eyes, that, she says—

then she mentions Dad, how he'd snatch
the watch from her hand and hold it up high
and say, It ticks! It ticks! She got a real
bargain, a real *matziah*, a Hamilton
that ticks! Then he'd parade around
the kitchen a little, do a kind of strut,
and she would grab the watch back from his
hand and strap it on her wrist and wear it
the rest of the day and say, I know! I know!
as if there wasn't any irony in his pronouncement
and who knows maybe there wasn't. That,
she says, mattered. And now, because
it's a dream, she grabs my wrist and zap!
we're in the house where he still lives, watching
him bend over a drawer with nine or ten
Seikos and Hamiltons, his forefinger
stirring them around as if they were morsels
of frying meat. He's speaking in a low voice:
She liked watches, your mother. So I ask her,
if the watches don't matter but this matters,
doesn't that mean that the watches matter?
She swirls her tumbler and we look up from
the kitchen counter at my dad who continues
explaining about watches, but soon all we hear
is the ticking of out-of-sync gears. Tick, tick, tick.

Something Forced

the amaryllis bulb. That's the verb we use:
forced it, its petals just one shade
more pleasing than blood. Do I mention

the year it lay dormant, or the spears'
thin green arrowheads, their announcement—
why not my mother's exhalation

beneath the pot, her ghostly avatar opening
its chalk line of a mouth, expelling what was once
breath into the bulb's white fist, coaxing

it open? And Dan—two dates in—
loved me. Briefly. Her entering him, too,
parting his shoulder blades like curtains, reaching

a vapor hand, finding and soothing the contours
of his heart like water running over clay: making
slip—that's the word, clay and its

diluted self, rounding, softening edges. The week
he loved me was good. If my mother's soul
couldn't do more than that, well, she got

the vessel turning. It wasn't unreasonable
to expect me to do the rest. What the cat sees
in her cat-staring? Something, certainly—

don't you, cat? Or hears, one ear rotating
outward, body otherwise still in a still

room. If I don't move—not even a breath—

that balance keeps: everything still but whisker
and soul dragging the gray lace of itself
across hardwood floors. When I told my mother

I'd bought acreage out in Ohio, she raised
an eyebrow and said, *I can't see you as much
of a farmer.* I guess we never had much

faith in each other. How can you see me, Ma?
Hard as I try, I can't see her as a soul. Not
some white transparence brushing

my cheeks. Silly me, thinking it the new
salve, Metrogel, finally clearing the rosacea
she and I shared on our similar faces. Anyway,

why would she look so closely after me
in death, when, in life, she never had?
When all she'd done—and in a selfish way,

a mostly selfish way—was love me?

"As Are Right Fit"

Because in her delirium, she raked my beard
with her nails and called me *aba*, I know
my mother traveled backwards into her death.
Because I leaned over her on the hospital bed
and had the presence of mind not to fear,
at least not then, being near her, I felt
the restlessness of her back-and-forth turning,
as of a body working itself into a narrow
channel or a groove, to rest, that cannot rest.
What she saw, where she was then, I can't
know—not from the bedrail where I stood
as if it were railing in a stadium, and I, high up,
watched her on the field below. Probably
she was in the Palestine of her childhood,
a location I will not try to imagine here.
She was twice removed from me, not simply
inside herself, but inside in a place before
I could have known her, where her needs,
her concerns had nothing to do with me,
and another middle-aged man with a beard
had leaned over her, leaned in to lift her
as from a crib, before he went off to war.
She'd said a few times that I resemble him
with my thick lips and straight hairline,
the features passed through her. So I went ahead.
I forgot what I thought I knew about time and
became the man who leaned over her once
returned to lean over her again, glad that,
in her delirium, she recognized me, her father-
son, light brown beard, thick lips, straight

hairline, and the creases around eyes and mouth
that are common to joy and grief.

Irreverent Though We Were, We Sang *Dayenu*

Had I asked in August, before the seizure, it would have been enough.

Had I asked in August, but not followed up about how you knew,

what in your body told you that the scope this time was different, that

you were, in fact, going to die, it would have been enough.

Had I asked about the difference in scope, but not how it felt to live

with that difference, the apron of it spread across your lap where

you always sat, mug in hand, paperback open, it would have been.

Had I asked what it was to sit with that difference, not cloth but

a lead apron, as for an x-ray, unwieldy for an old woman, but not

asked if you were afraid—weren't you, Ma, afraid?—it would have been.

Asked about your fear and not been silent so you could answer.

Been silent as you answered, but not asked how you were sleeping

when you couldn't talk about this with Dad, with Gina, me, or anyone.

Asked how you were sleeping, but not driven down next morning

with whatever cellophane-wrapped ShopRite flowers, whatever cheaply

manufactured brightness that is still, God help us, a brightness.

Come down with flowers, but not settled in beside you on the couch, not watched *Big Bang Theory* reruns all afternoon, making no more

of my trip down than I-had-the-day-why-not-I-had-the-day? brought you

half a toasted bagel when you wanted it, or more coffee, or a tissue,

had I, it would have been. Sat beside you and still not really

heard the hardening in your voice, the *not doing well, not well*

in its gravity, my palm flat against yours, sitting on the couch,

there are times, aren't there, when an adult man can still

hold his mother's hand? Had I heard fully and let you know

I heard the scope of what you were saying, it would have been

enough. And that simple touch might have done it.

Months Later, Even

in public, my shaking head, muttering *You
sons of bitches*. I hear myself and wonder
what I am. Some wad

of mismatched fiber, maybe. I'm talking, I know,
to her doctors and nurses, I mean
the oncologist who

after a month of trying I finally got on the phone
a few days before she—and when
I asked about restarting

immunotherapy he said only, *Her prognosis
isn't good*, as if we were both doctors conferring
in a hallway over files. No,

not *prognosis*. The word you want is *mother*, please
reformulate your sentence to include
the word *mother*,

you son of a bitch, I didn't say before handing
the phone over to my father who
thanked him for taking our call

on a Sunday. In the bland, vanilla hospital
light, she, patient with a prognosis,
lay four-hours silent. At one point

I wandered to the nurses' station to sift through
the drugs she was getting. Something
about her stomach, her not

being fed in three days. Why not? How much
energy do you expect her to have if she's
not being fed, you

—well I didn't say any of that, but wondered
how, half-conscious in bed, she'd know
if she were dying or merely

feeling like it. And how to have the will to get better
if she didn't know? Here's
a sentimental detail: I brought

a stuffed rabbit, powder blue fur with a silver-stitching
nose, laid it against her shoulder but didn't
object or place it back when

nurses came to turn her, didn't object even when
my brother cut himself a thick slice
of the pound cake he'd brought

because—all day in the hospital—though, for her,
it had been three days. I watched him, my gut
a flaring match head, that initial

susurrant flush. Looking back, I wish I'd held out
my arms, spun like hilltop Julie Andrews, become
a top that yanked down

separating curtains, hanging transfusion bags,
stands. Toppled a few hallway carts, too. Not
like a top, but a funnel

cloud; not hands open, but alternating grabbing
with fists. Think Tasmanian Devil, think guards
taking steps two at a time to

the fifth floor, to what they call "Critical
Care," their hands reaching to their
holsters as they run. *Now,*

I might have insisted, *I want some goddamn
answers right now, you sons of*
—and then I could have said it. Just then.

Seeing Those Damn Greasy

circa 2016

day-old chickens, hunched, roasted,
and stacked in clear
plastic domes
in a refrigerated case by the checkout
compel of all people God
help me my mother

who sashays over, purse swinging,
to their round half-off
stickers, and one
by one lifts each, closely
inspecting the trussed, browned
limbs therein, sometimes

bringing the plastic seam
of a package right up against her nose,
all the while describing much
much too loudly how a whole
chicken is dinner for two nights, and
what's left can be

shredded from the breast
for her salad, that you can't
go wrong, not for three dollars, *you
simply can't go wrong*—
this was back before
the diagnosis, before I saw

her face, her lips, barely differentiated

grays, her lying on the end
of a couch, tiny
under afghans, and realized,
only in retrospect realized, that she was
looking at me with what was really

a kind of startled wonder
as if trying to
account for me, for how such a large
busyness had emerged
whole from her body, and it was also
before I learned

as I did after she died
that she had in accounts
not even my father
knew about, money almost no calculus
of parsimony could explain, no
daily palm sweeping

off the kitchen table from among
keys, wallet, and phone,
my father's change, no part-
time work, which she did, as a nurse,
for twenty years, money
enough to buy cartloads

of chickens, chickens prepared
special, whole platters of chickens fresh
from the deli counter—
makes me want, there
in the ShopRite, to retract
into myself, my arms, electric

car antennae drawing back into
my sleeves, my head sinking tortoise-like
into the shell
of my torso, makes me want,
though I do understand, theoretically,
that a day may come when

a minute with her, even one of such
flaming public embarrassment,
will be as far from my grasp as
any culture's
vision of heaven, makes me
want, right there on the spot, to

wink out like a soap bubble, a perfect
sphere of swirling color
poked by a child's finger.

Yahrzeit

Then one for my grandmother, who, with a paring knife, used to dig
        remaining wax from the small jars
the following afternoon, hard scrapes that even as a child I understood
        were a bad idea,

the sharp blade careening up the sides of the glass. Sometimes she held
        a jar under the steaming tap
as she scraped, and spurts of blood seemed inevitable. But a day or two
        later, they would be stacked

in her built-in cupboards—the cabinet doors repainted so many times,
        so thickly yellow, they no longer
closed. When, in the middle of the night, she brought me water, it arrived
        in those jars.

She'd have stood proudly behind me in her brown cardigan and long
        wool skirt as I light these candles, stood as if
we were all about to go to *schul*, her wrinkly hands clasping one another,
        lipstick on a few of her front teeth.

She'd be wearing a rose-gold bracelet from the old country, bought when
        she prepared to emigrate, the conversion
of all her worldly pelf. In fact, she's almost here now, nodding as I hold
        the match. In her post-death knowing, maybe

she accepts that one of the candles is for a dog. Accepts—as I lift the
        glass, reach down with a wooden
match, flames licking up along it right to my thumb and forefinger—
        that another is for a *shiksa*.

She understands more about acceptance now, among the dead. And loss.
        She even finds a spiritual charge
in her insistence on reusing the jars. But, as I light the last candle, your
        candle, the one for her only

daughter, her lips tighten like they used to when I'd refuse to run the
        hard plastic teeth of her blue comb over my
head, and she'd grab it and do it herself, scratching—intentionally it
        seemed—my scalp. I lower the match

until the wick catches and a small glow fills the jar. Don't worry, I want
        to tell her, I'll set this one aside, too—
after the light burns itself out. I'll rinse it with water from the kettle until
        the wax drains and the glass clears.

She Approves

It was not evening-out jewelry,
not twice-a-year jewelry.
She slept in it. She always said
when she died I would have it
but almost certainly never
pictured me wearing it:
how it would lie an inch
below my beard, in the hollow
between my clavicles,
how the serpentine chain
would catch stray hairs
on my shoulders and neck
and the emerald bright
with its corona of diamond chips
would fill the open collar
of a flannel shirt, over jeans,
brown belt, work boots, and be,
to the right kind of man, a signal—
a traffic light glowing green
at the most vulnerable spot
on my throat. Now in death,
she understands the necklace
was always about drawing the eye
to the flesh: a way to scoop
light from the air, to make
a man want to catch that light
like a snowflake on his tongue.
Yes. That's the word
she's saying to the body
most like her own once was,

briefly incarnating herself
in front of me to straighten
the chain. My mother like
any mother willing her child
to be beautiful: *Yes, it fits
like that, close to your throat.*

My Husband and Mother Meet

In the softness of river silt. In cold water
          rushing past my ankles, as my toes
sink. In a dream of two doors across from
          each other, opening inward. In a mouth
like a bite of chocolate followed by a swallow
          of strong coffee. In a tree like jay and robin
alighting simultaneously on the same branch
          and together waiting out its trembling.
Like air masses, hot and cold, with lightning
          erupting at the seam, sparking a line
of storms that sweeps through a state
          on its way out to the ocean. Like an ocean
and the bed in which it rocks: each
          shaping each to itself. In a dream
in which I watch like the eye of God
          Blake saw looking in through his window,
green iris contracting in the mullions.
          And listen like the ear of God that Blake
didn't see, pressed against an exterior wall
          to hear if they are talking about me.
On a plate, run together: two dishes both
          sweet and salty, that make each other
sweeter and bring out each other's salt.
          Across the table in a restaurant, the space
between filled with the movement of hands.
          In the imagination Theseus imagined
in which shapes are scared up from
          airy nothing, and that which Lady Macbeth
demonstrated, in which they come back
          from the inky spill of death. In dreams:

the sleeping kind no less than the aspirational,
	and the reddened, knotting flesh
where they heal together. At her funeral,
	I'd have been holding his hand.
And when I daydream a husband, imagine
	our wedding, she's there. She comes over,
vodka tonic swaying in her fingers,
	to peck his cheek, then caress mine.

Acknowledgments

My thanks to the journals in which these poems first appeared, sometimes in earlier versions:

> *Asheville Poetry Review*: "My Husband and Mother Meet" and "The Poem as an Act of Betrayal"
>
> *Barrow Street*: "The Auction"
>
> *Boulevard*: "Trying to Bathe a Kitten, My Brothers Drown It"
>
> *Chattahoochee Review*: "My Mother's Dying"
>
> *Colorado Review*: "Yahrzeit"
>
> *december*: "My Mother's Charm Bracelet"
>
> *Denver Quarterly*: "Pre/Post" and "Vigil"
>
> *Mid-American Review*: "I Sit at Her Bedside"
>
> *Ploughshares*: "My Mother Approves"
>
> *River Styx*: "Seeing Those Damn Greasy"
>
> *Southern Indiana Review*: "Irreverent Though We Were, We Sang Dayenu"
>
> *Southern Poetry Review*: "Mother Pulls Closed"
>
> *The Tusculum Review*: "Months Later, Even"
>
> *The Yale Review*: "Something Forced," "The Wedgwood, the Watches," and "'As Are Right Fit'"

"Seeing Those Damn Greasy" was republished on *Verse Daily*, 11/15/2022.

"My Mother Approves" was reprinted in *Braving the Body* (Harbor Anthologies, 2024).

"Mother Pulls Closed" was reprinted in a *Southern Poetry Review* retrospective, 61.2.

I'm deeply grateful to friends who lent their support: Steve Green, Lukas Lesnewski, Clare Rossini, Paul Simmons, Bryan Sinche, Julien Strong, Steven R. Young, and the poets of Brickwalk. Thanks also to Eliza Carlson, Kristiane Weeks-Rogers, Allison Blevins, and the rest of the folks at Harbor Editions for their patience and for making me such a beautiful book. And finally, my gratitude to the University of Hartford for helping me get these poems into the world and to Jacqueline Osherow for her generous words.

About the Author

Originally from Far Rockaway, New York, Benjamin S. Grossberg was educated at Rutgers and the University of Houston. From 2000 to 2008, he worked at Antioch College in Ohio, where he purchased a small farm and planted the Granny Smith orchard for which his second book was named. He is currently Director of Creative Writing and a Professor of English at the University of Hartford, in Hartford, Connecticut.

Ben's previous books of poetry include *My Husband Would* (University of Tampa Press, 2020), winner of the Connecticut Book Award and a Foreword INDIES Book of the Year; *Space Traveler* (University of Tampa Press, 2014); *Sweet Core Orchard* (University of Tampa Press, 2009), winner of the Tampa Review Prize and a Lambda Literary Award; and *Underwater Lengths in a Single Breath* (Ashland Poetry Press, 2007), winner of the Snyder Prize. He has also published two chapbooks, *An Elegy* (Jacar Press, 2016) and *The Auctioneer Bangs his Gavel* (Kent State University Press, 2006). He co-edited an anthology, *The Poetry of Capital* (University of Wisconsin Press, 2020), which curates poems about the economic pressures of our moment. And he wrote the novel, *The Spring before Obergefell* (University of Nebraska Press, 2024), selected by Percival Everett for the 2023 AWP Award Series James Alan McPherson Prize.

Ben is also a runner, vegetarian, and cat steward.

About Small Harbor Publishing

Small Harbor Publishing is a 501c3 nonprofit organization. Our goal is to publish unique and diverse voices. We are a feminist press, and we are committed to diversity and inclusion. We strive to bring new voices to a devoted and expanding readership.

Small Harbor Publishing began in 2018 with the first issue of *Harbor Review*. The magazine is an online space where poetry and art converse. *Harbor Review* quickly grew and now publishes reviews and runs multiple micro chapbook competitions, including the Washburn Prize and the Editor's Prize.

In July 2020, Small Harbor Publishing was officially incorporated and began Harbor Editions. Harbor Editions accepts submissions through a chapbook open reading period, a hybrid chapbook open reading period, the Marginalia Series, and the Laureate Prize.

In 2023, Harbor Anthologies began with a mission to promote texts that explore social justice issues and highlight marginalized writers.

If you would like to support Small Harbor Publishing, please visit our "About" page at smallharborpublishing.com/about.